Baby Sign Language
Official Reference Dictionary

Table of Contents

Introduction

The Baby Sign Language Dictionary includes more than 600 of the most commonly used signs in Baby Sign Language. We suggest using this book in conjunction with our online video dictionary (www.BabySignLanguage.com/dictionary), particularly when learning a sign for the first time. We find that the online videos better convey the signing motion, while the diagrams better convey finger positioning.

The signs used in this book are American Sign Language (ASL), which is the predominant sign language in the United States. Certain signs in this dictionary may be depicted differently in other books or by other ASL users. This is due to the existence of several acceptable variations for many words in ASL. For signs with variations, we provide the simplest option.

Should you need a word not found in this dictionary, consult a comprehensive ASL dictionary (e.g., www.ASLpro.com or www.lifeprint.com).

Left and Right Handed Signing

The illustrations in the dictionary are based on right handed signing. When signing, your dominant hand plays the starring role and your non-dominant hand plays the supporting role. If you are right handed, the action part of the sign will be formed with your right hand. If you are left handed, the left hand will do most of the action and the right hand will play the supporting role.

You may reverse hands if it is more convenient. For example, if you are right handed and holding your baby with your right hand, feel free to sign with your left hand.

Conventions

Two or more diagrams are provided for each sign. The first (left-most) diagram shows the starting position for your hands and indicates the direction of motion. The final diagram shows the ending position for your hands. Let's use *cat* as an example.

Cat

| **Starting Position and Motion** | **Ending Position** |

To sign *cat*, start with your dominant hand by the side of your face, with your thumb and index finger extended (left diagram). From that starting point, bring your thumb and index finger together, then move your hand away from your face (right diagram). The *cat* sign resembles a person pulling on a whisker.

Comments are welcome. E-mail us at dictionary@babysignlanguage.com, connect with us through our website at www.BabySignLanguage.com, or join our Facebook community at www.facebook.com/babysignlang.

Aa

A

Adult

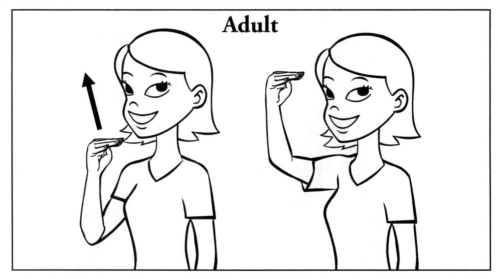

Afraid

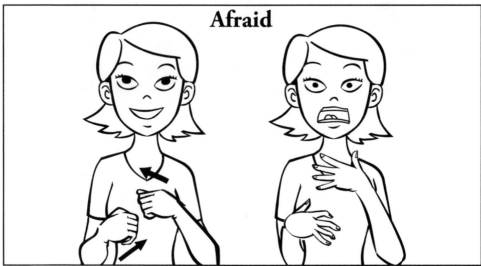

Again

Airplane

All Done

All Gone

Alligator

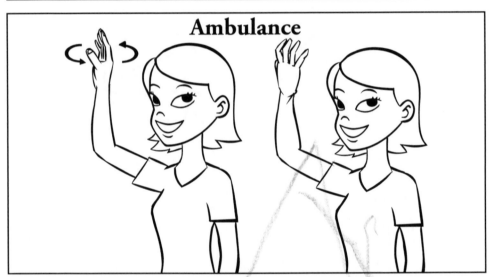

Ambulance

Angry

Animal

Ant

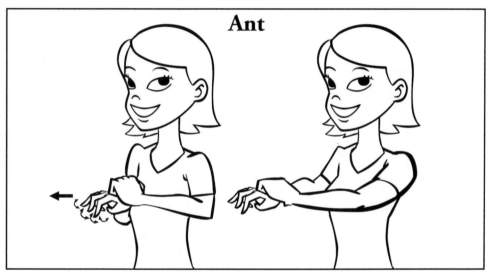

Apple

Art

Aunt

Avocado

Bb

B

Baby

Babysitter

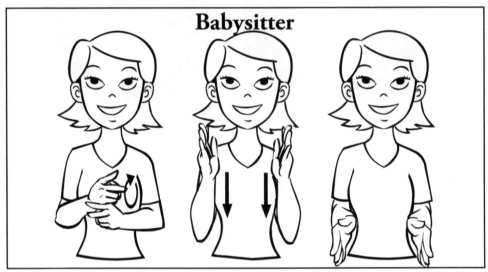

Backpack

Bacon

Bad

Bag

Ball

Balloon

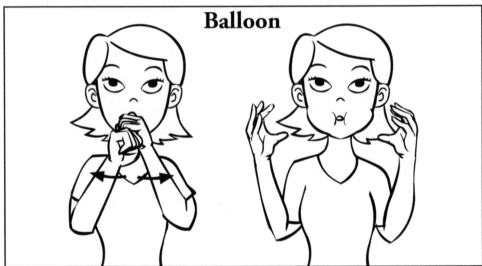

Banana

Bandage

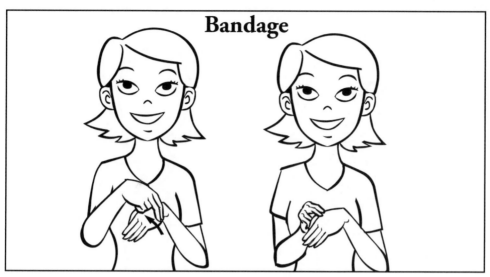

Basement

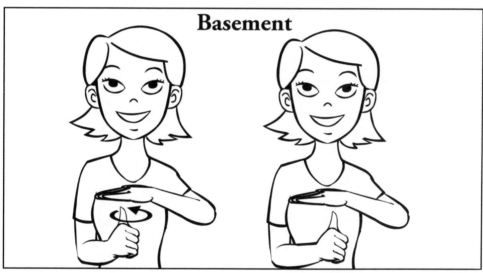

Bath

Battery

Be Careful

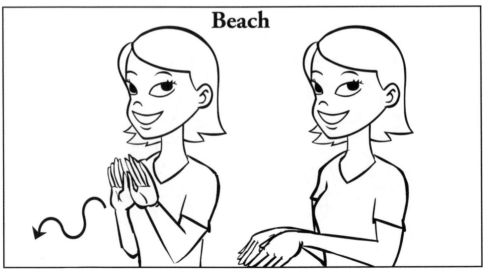

Beach

Bean

Bear

Beautiful

Bed

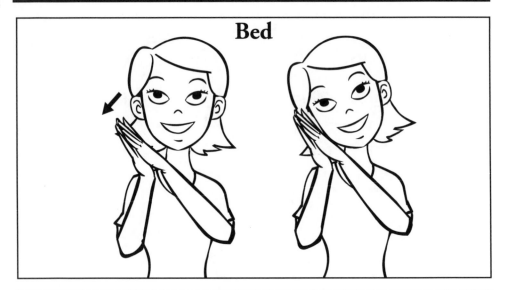

Bedroom

Bee

Behave

Bell

Belt

Bib

Bicycle

Big

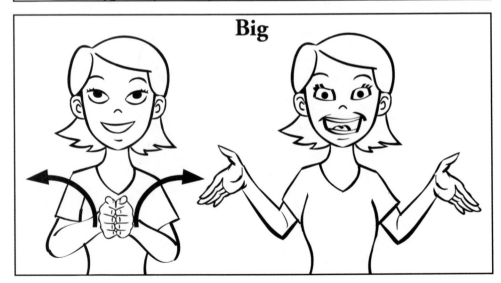

Bird

Birthday

Bite

Black

Blanket

Blocks

Blonde

Blue

Blueberry

Boat

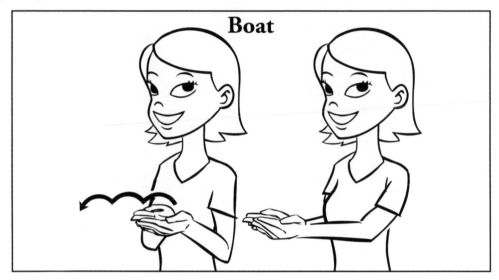

Book

Boots

Bottle

Bowl

Box

Boy

Bracelet

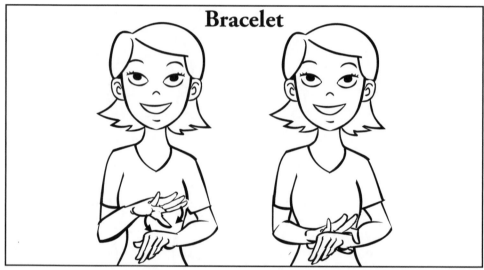

Branch

Bread

Breakfast

Breast Feed

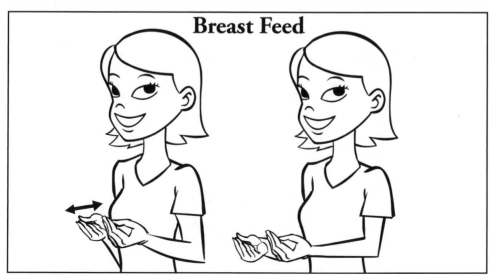

Breast Milk

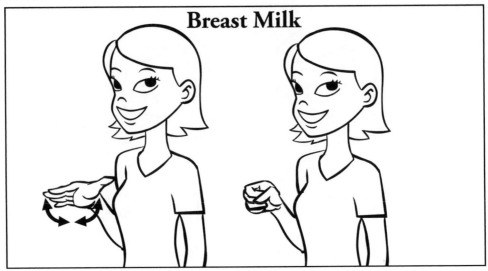

Broken

Brother

Brown

Bubbles

Bucket

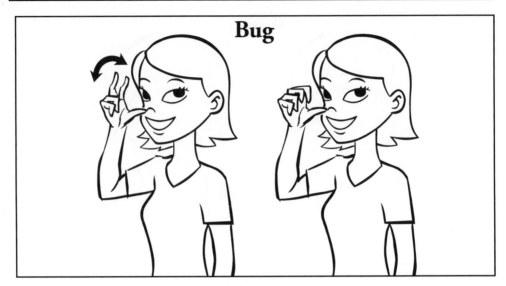

Bus

Busy

Butter

Butterfly

Button

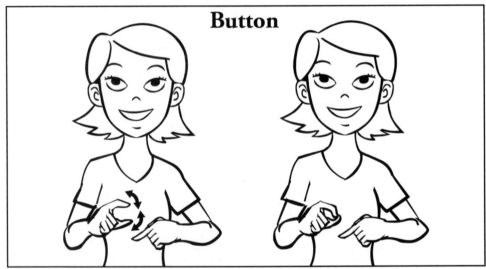

Bye Bye

C

Cage

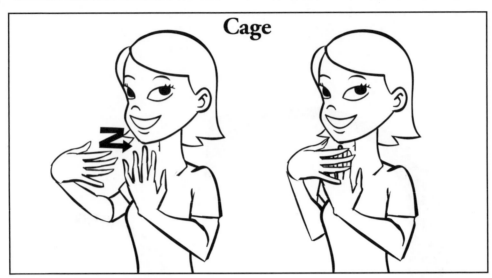

Cake

Camera

Candle

Candy

Car

Cards

Careful

Cat

Caterpillar

Cereal

Chair

Change

Cheese

Cherry

Chicken

Children

Chocolate

Christmas

Church

Circle

Class

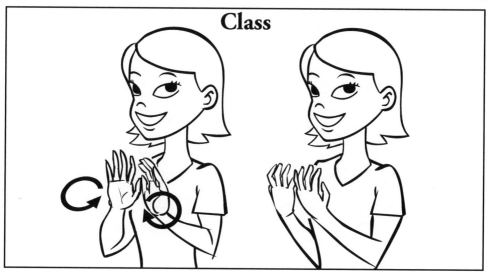

Closet

Clothes

Cloud

Clown

Coat

Cold

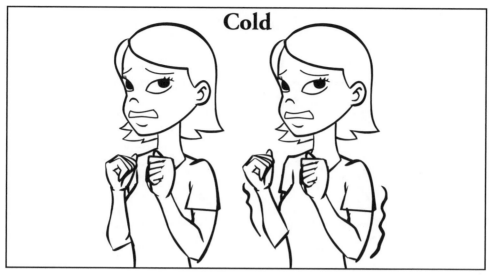

Color

Come

Computer

Cook

Cookie

Corn

Count

Cousin

Cow

Crab

Cracker

Crawl

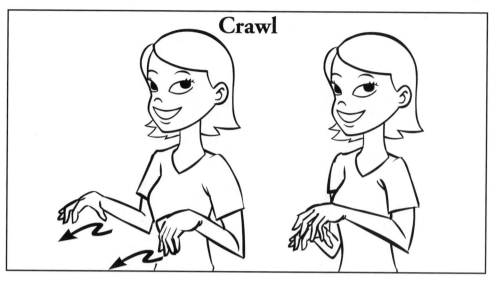

Cry

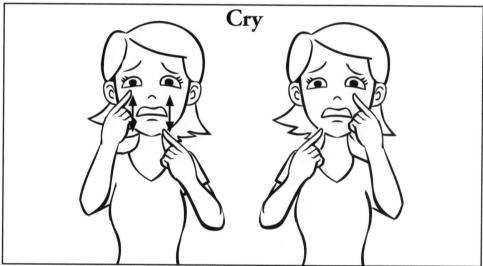

Cup

Cupboard

Cut

Cute

Dd

D

Daddy

Dance

Dark

Day

Deer

Dentist

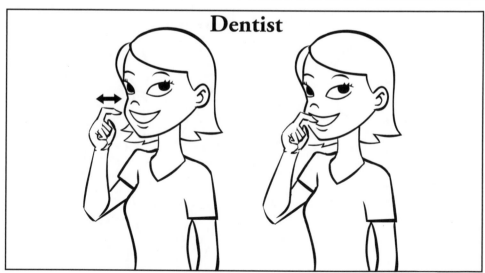

Dessert

Diaper

Dining Room

Dinner

Dinosaur

Dirt / Dirty

Doctor

Dog

Doll

Dolphin

Don't

Don't Hit

Don't Know

Don't Like

Don't Want

Door

Doorbell

Down

Dress (garment)

Dress (get dressed)

Drink

Drum

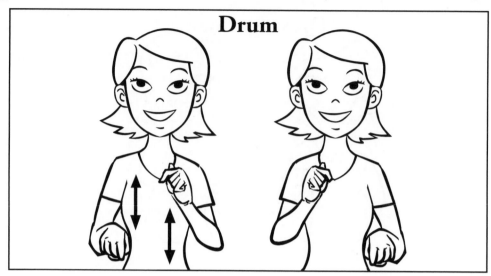

Dry

Duck

E e

E

Earphone

Earring

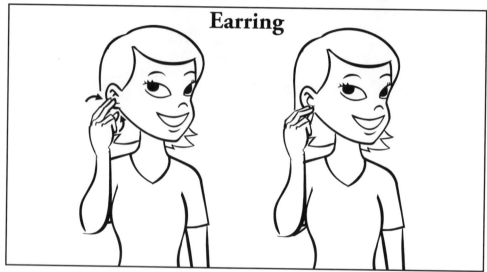

Easter

Eat

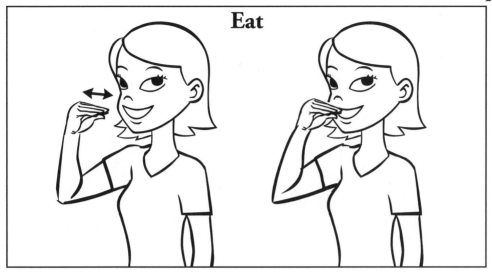

Egg

Elephant

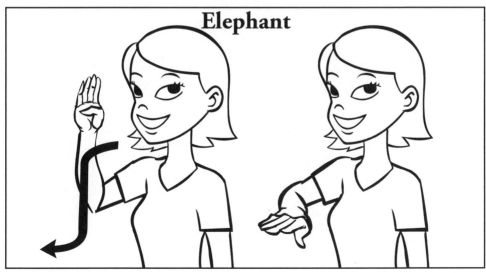

Excited

Excuse Me

Eyeglasses

Ff

F

Fall Down

Family

Fan

Farm

Farmer

Fast

Fat

Favorite

Feather

Feel

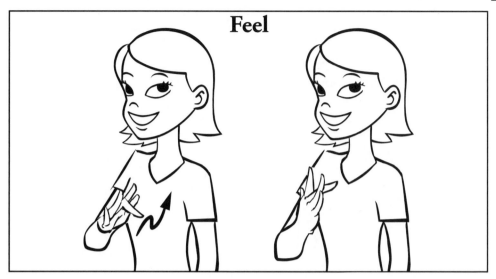

Feet

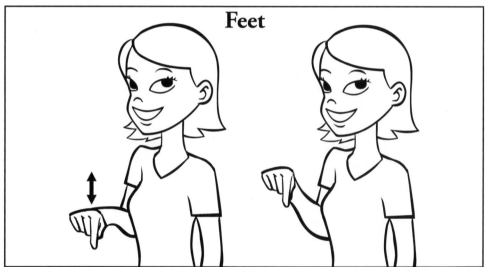

Ferret

Find

Fire

Firefighter

Fireworks

Fireworks (continued)

Fish

Fix

Flag

Flashlight

Floor

Flower

Fork

Fox

French Fries

Friend

Frog

Fruit

Frustrated

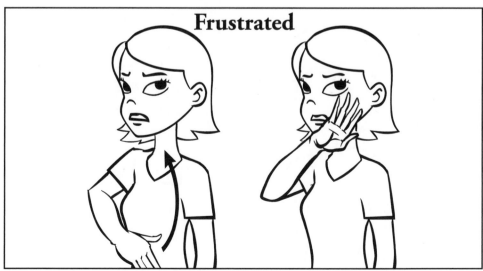

Full

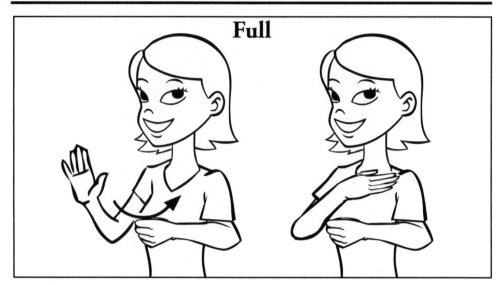

Fun

Funny

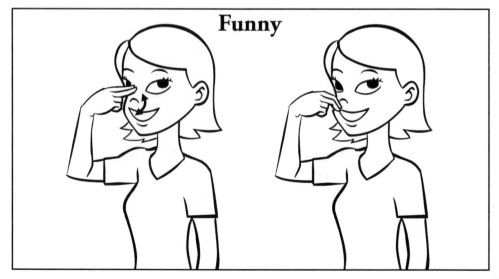

Gg

G

Game

Garage

Garbage

Garden

Gate

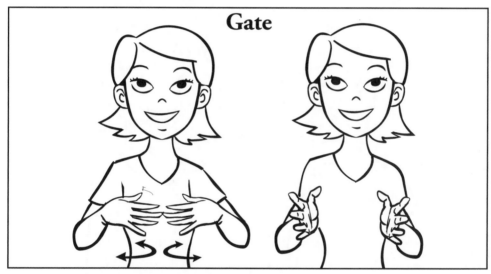

Gentle

Gift

Giraffe

Girl

Give

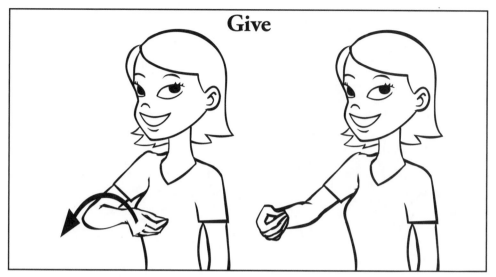

Gloves

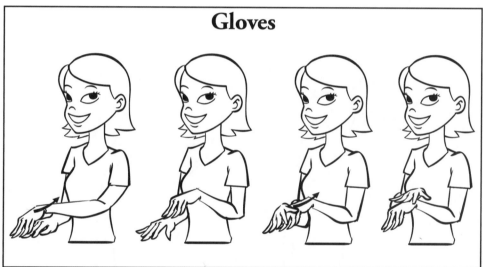

Glue

Go

Goat

Good

Good Morning

Good Night

Goose

Gorilla

Grandfather

Grandmother

Grapes

Grass

Gray

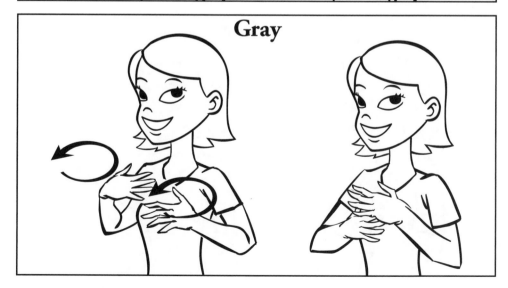

Green

Grumpy

Guitar

Hh

H

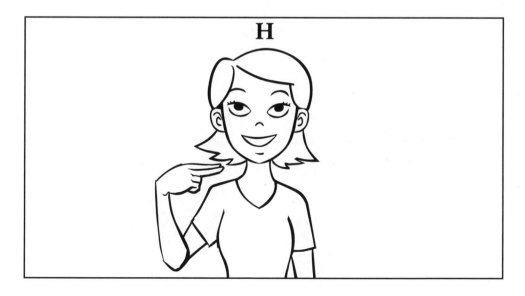

Hair

Hair Brush (brush hair)

Hall

Hamburger

Hanukkah

Happy

Hat

Hear

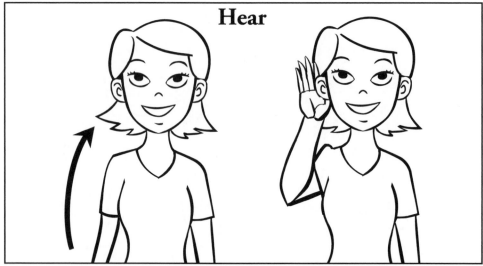

Heart

Helicopter

Hello

Help

High

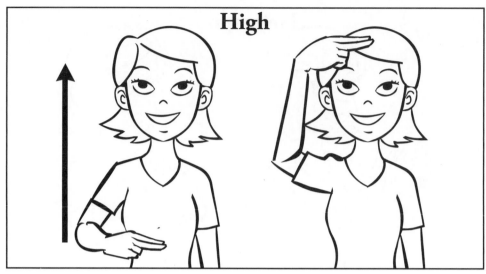

Hill

Hippopotamus

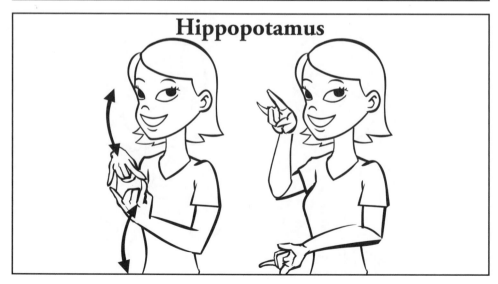

Hit

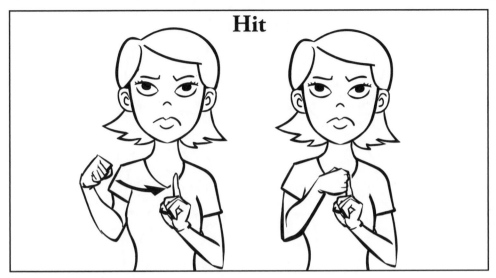

Holiday

Horse

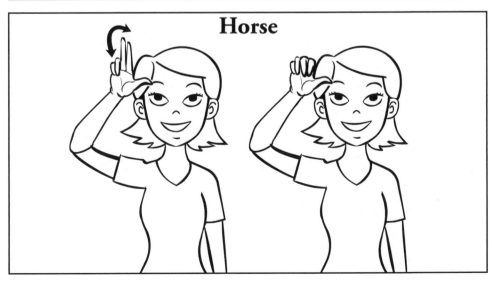

Hospital

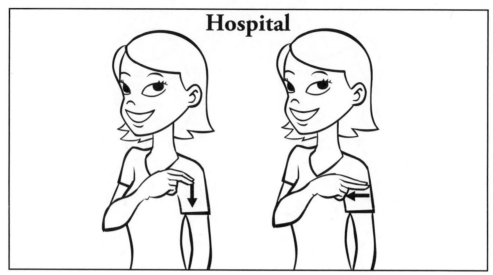

Hot

Hotdog

House

How

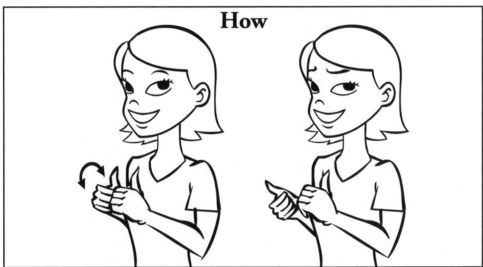

Hug

Hungry

Hurry

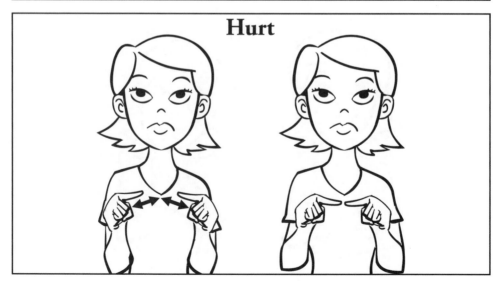

Hurt

Ii

I

I Love You

Ice

Ice Cream

In

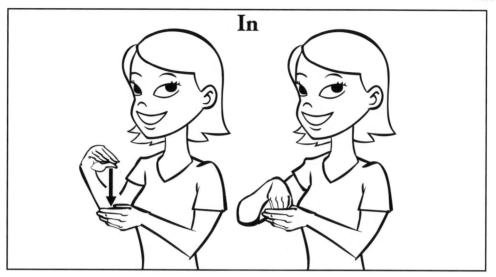

Inside

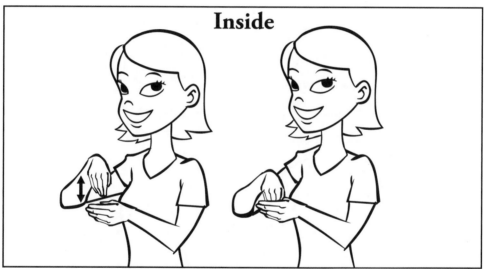

Internet

Ipad

Island

Itch

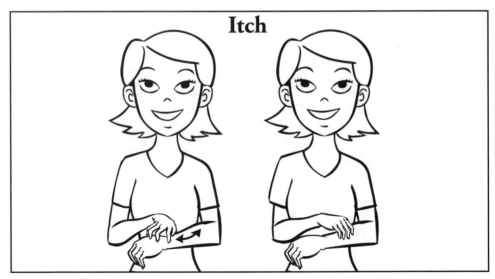

Jj

J

Jelly (jam)

Juice

Jump

Kk

K

Kangaroo

Keys

Kick

King

Kiss

Kitchen

Kite

Knife

Koala

L l

L

Ladder

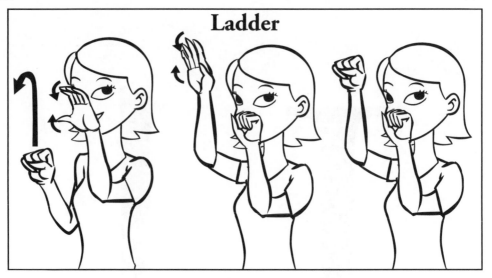

Lake

Lamb

Later

Laugh

Laundry

Leaf

Lemon

Letter

Lettuce

Library

Light

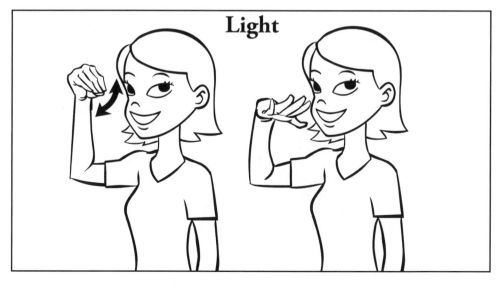

Like

Lion

List

Little

Llama

Long

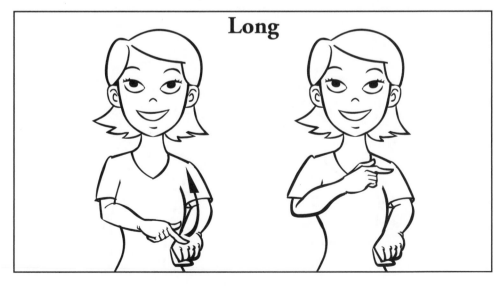

Look At

Love

Lunch

Mm

M

Mad

Magazine

Magic

Magnet

Make

Man

Many

Mask

Meat

Medicine

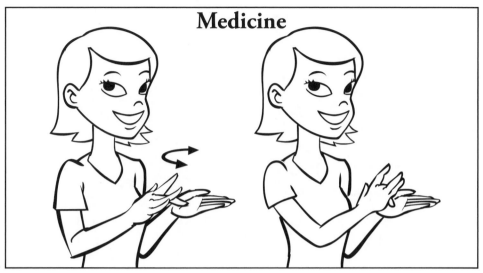

Melon

Messy

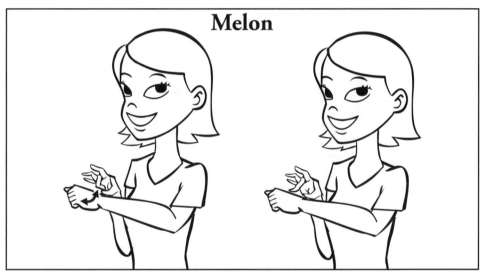

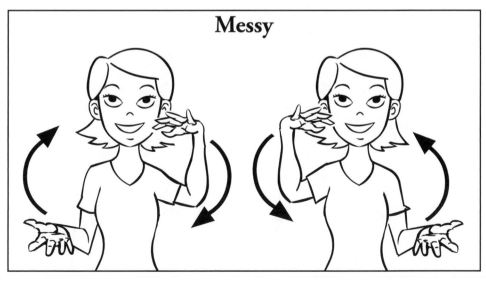

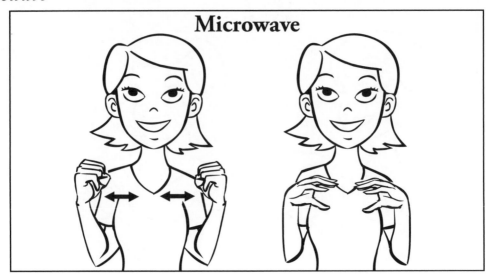

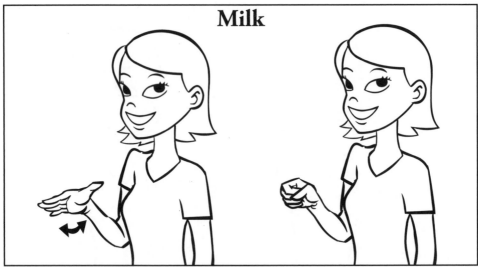

Mommy

Money

Monkey

Monster

Moon

Moose

More

Motorcycle

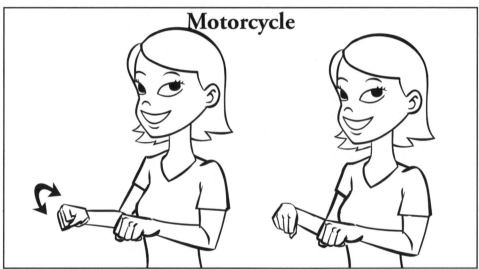

Mouse

Movie

Mushroom

Music

Nn

Naked

Nanny

Napkin

Near

Necklace

Necktie

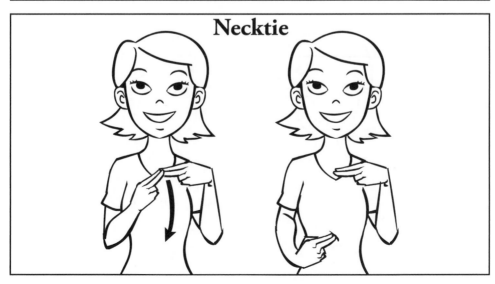

Nice (clean)

Niece

Night

Nightmare

No

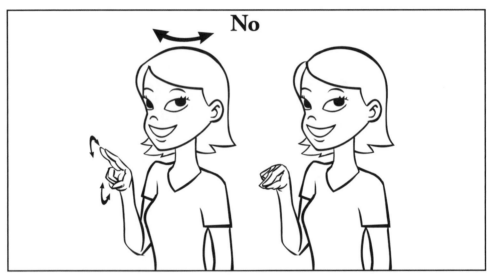

Noise

None

Nose

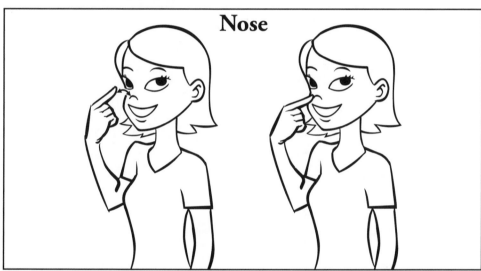

Now

Number

Nurse

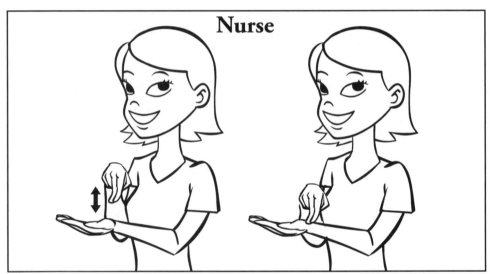

Nut

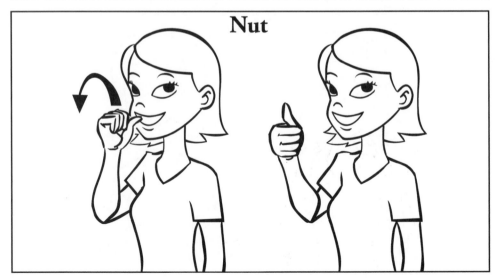

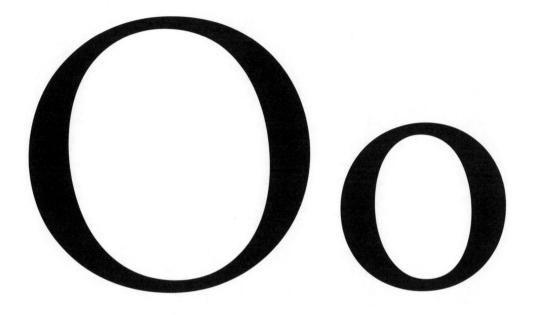

O

Ocean

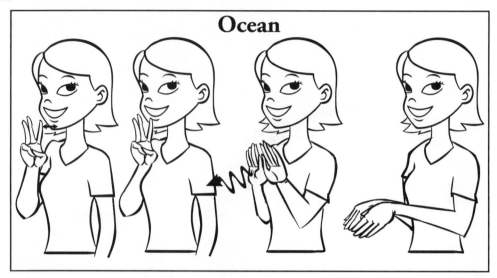

Octopus

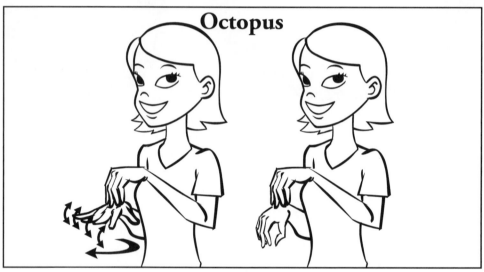

Off

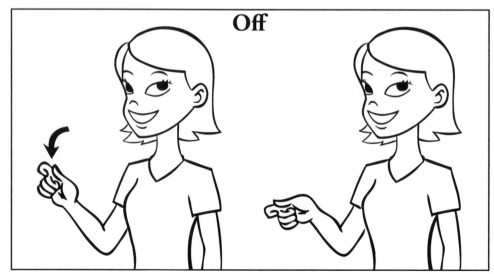

Office

Okay

Old

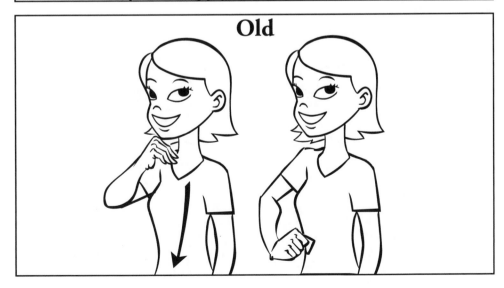

On

Onion

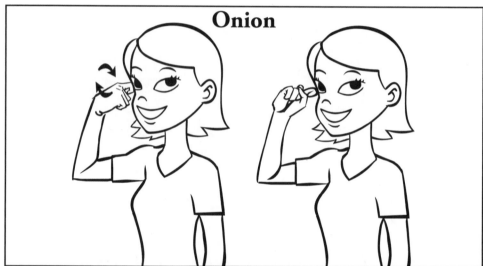

Open

Orange

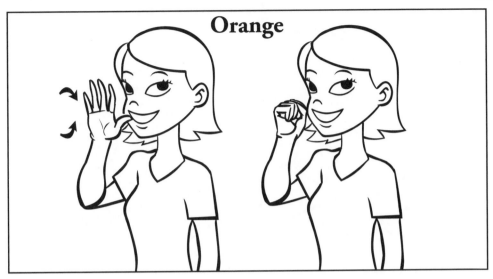

Out

Outside

Oven

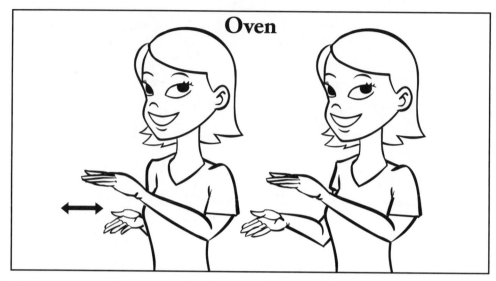

Over

Owl

P p

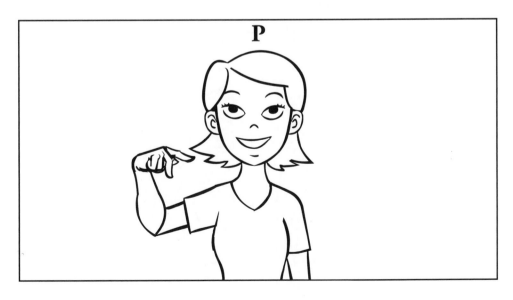

P

Pacifier

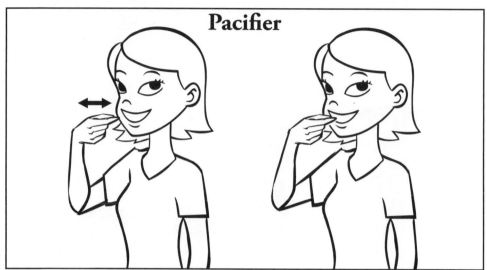

Paint

Pajamas

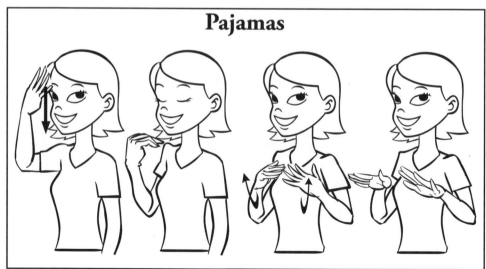

Pancake

Panda

Pants

Paper

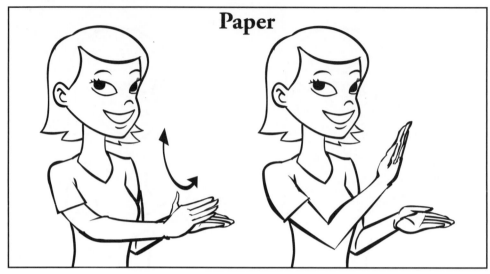

Park

Party

Pasta

Peach

Peanut Butter

Pear

Peas

Pee

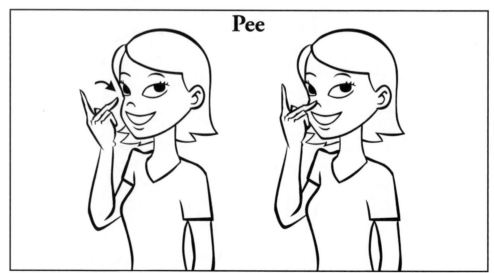

Pen

Phone

Photograph

Piano

Pickle

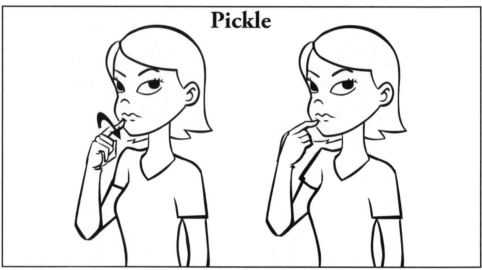

Picnic

Pig

Pillow

Pineapple

Pink

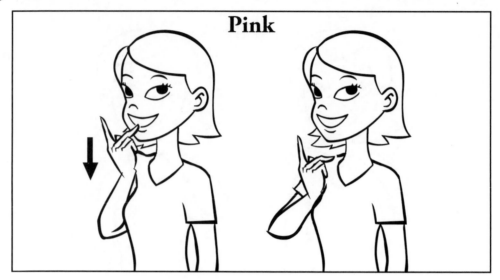

Pizza

Plant

Plate

Play

Playground

Please

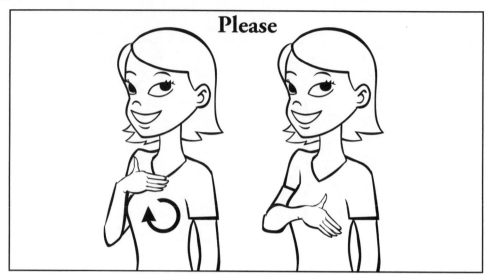

Plug

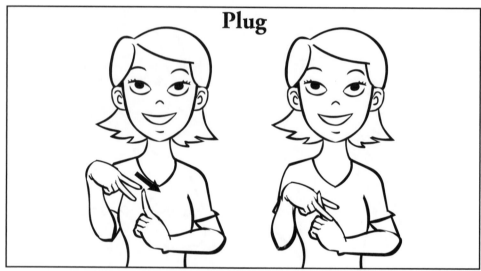

Pocket

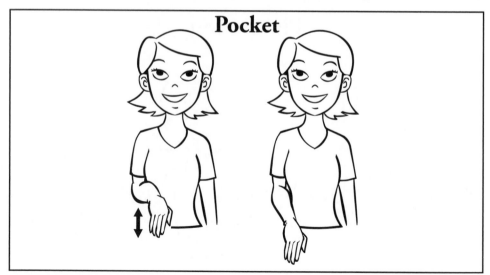

Police

Poop

Popcorn

Pot

Potato

Potty

President

Pretzel

Prince

Princess

Proud

Pull

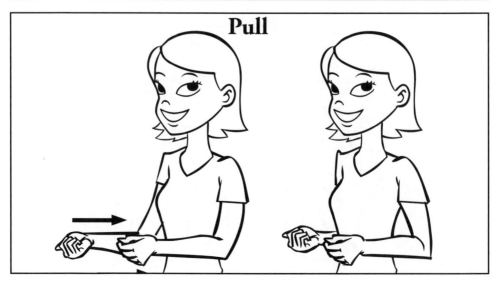

Pumpkin

Puppet

Purple

Push

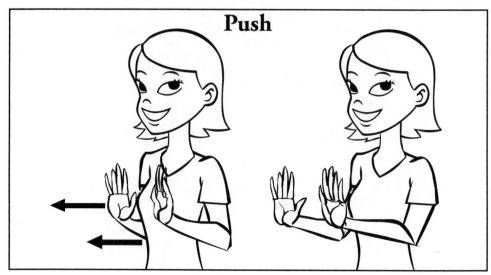

Put On

Puzzle

Q

Queen

Quick

Quiet

Rr

R

Raccoon

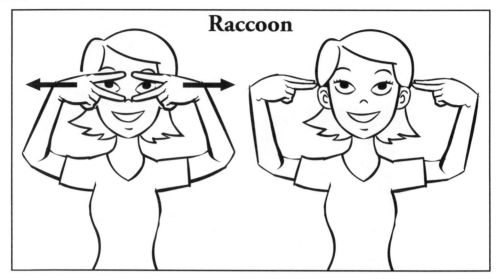

Radio

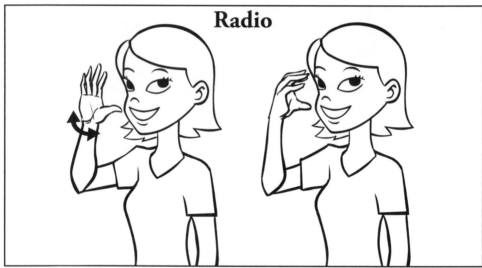

Rain

Rainbow

Rat

Rattle

Read

Ready

Rectangle

Red

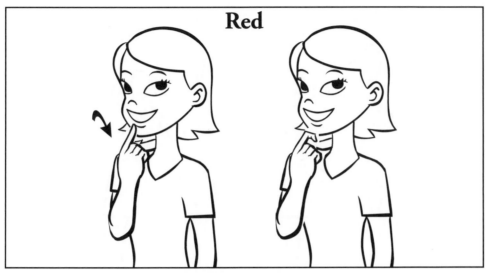

Refrigerator

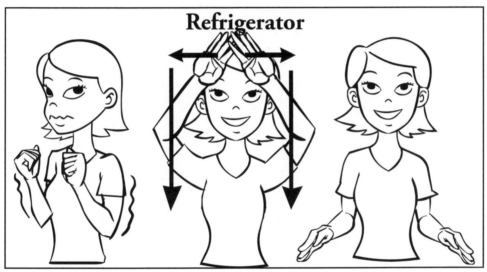

Reptile

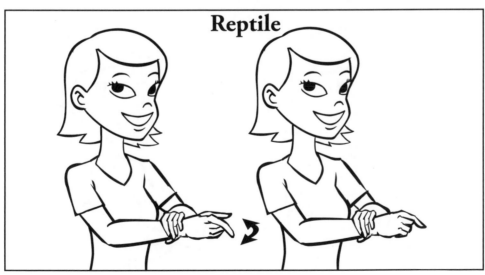

Restaurant

Rice

Ride

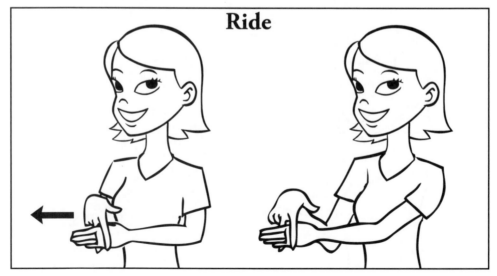

Ring

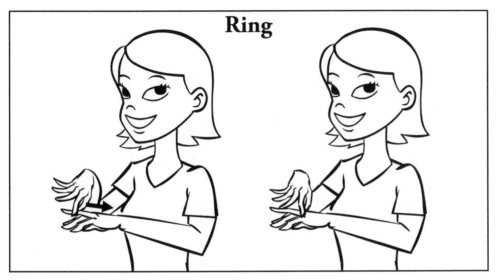

River

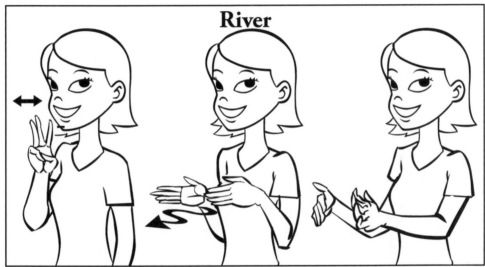

Rock

Roof

Rope

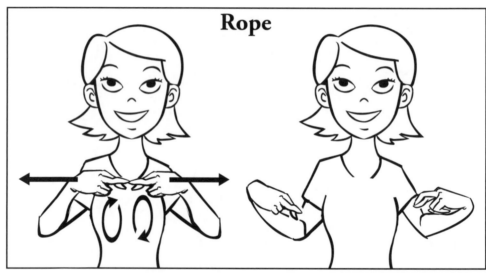

Run

Ss

S

Sad

Salad

Salt

Same

Sandwich

School

Scissors

Seal

See

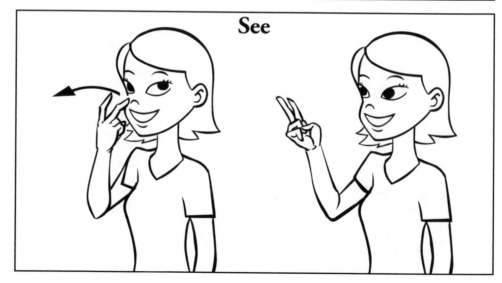

Shampoo

Share

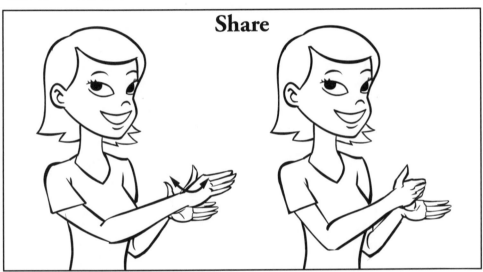

Shark

Sheep

Shirt

Shoes

Short

Shower

Shrimp

Shy

Sick

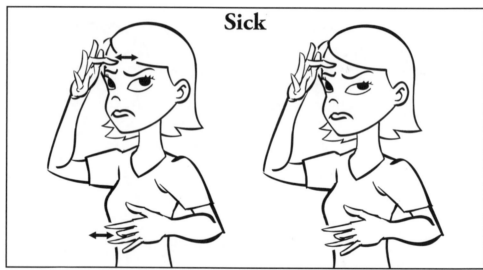

Sign (Sign Language)

Sing

Sink

Sister

Sit

Skate (ice skate)

Skate (roller skate)

Ski

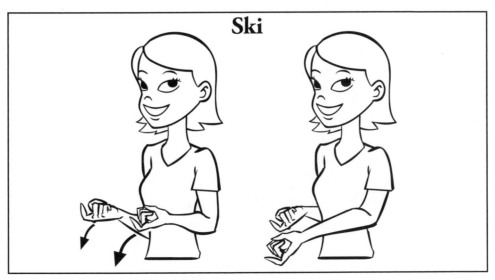

Skunk

Sky

Sled

Sleep

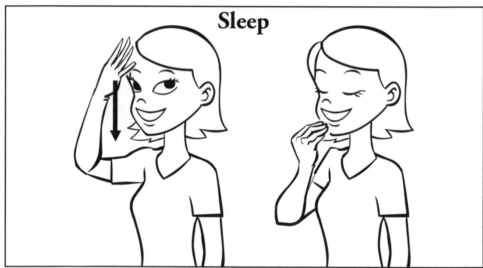

Slide

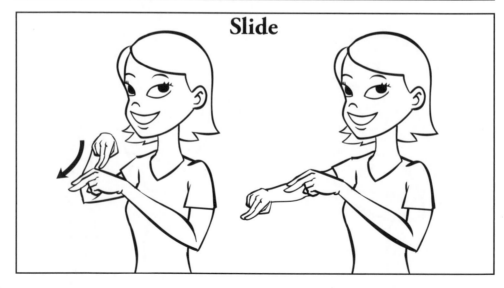

Slow

Smart

Smell

Smile

Snack

Snake

Sneeze

Snow

Soap

Socks

Sofa

Sorry

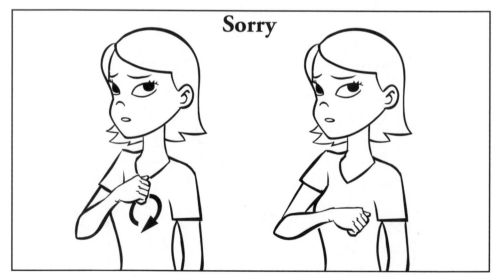

Soup

Sour

Spell

Spider

Spill

Sponge

Spoon

Square

Squirrel

Stairs

Stand

Stars

Start

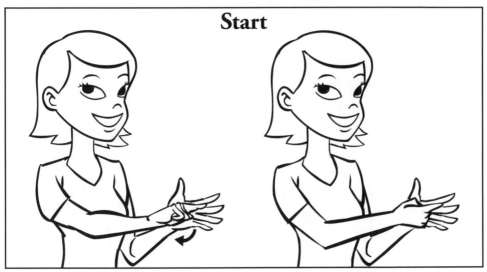

Stick

Sticky

Stinky

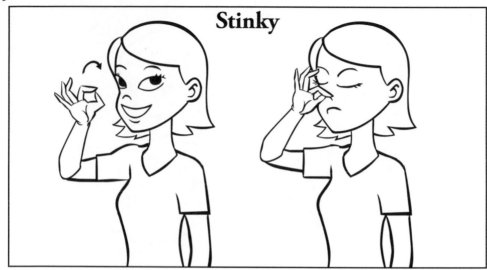

Stop

Store

Strawberry

Street

Stroller

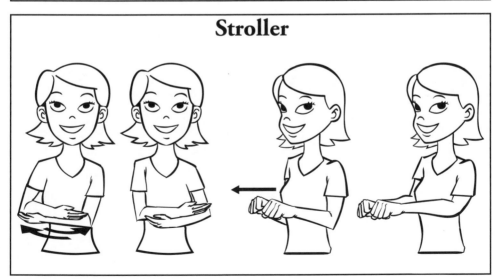

Strong

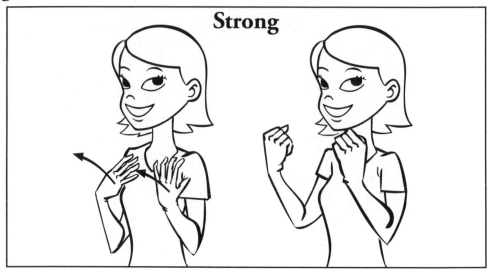

Sugar (sweet)

Sun

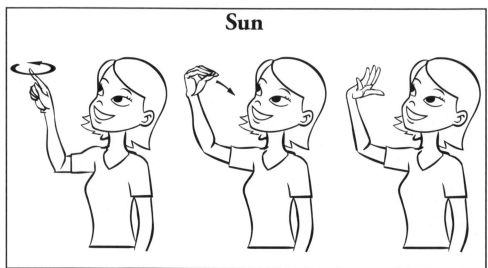

Supermarket

Surprise

Sweater

Sweep

Swim

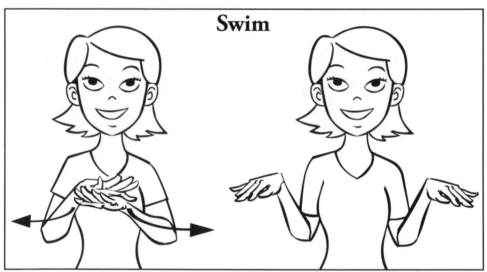

Swing

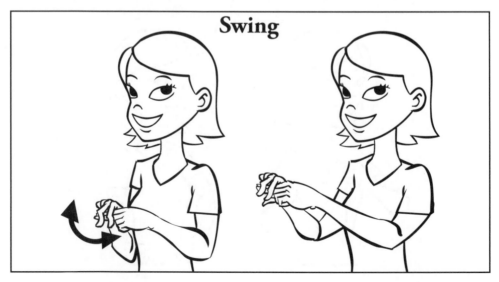

T t

T

Table

Talk

Tall

Tape

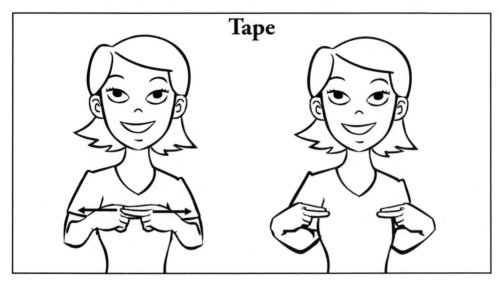

Taste

Taxi

Teacher

Television

Tell

Tent

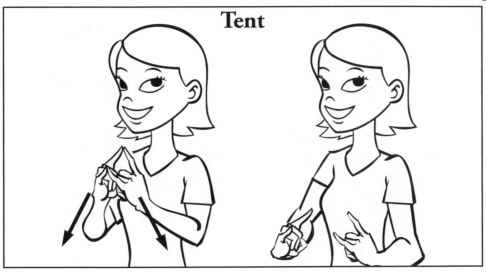

Thank You

Thanksgiving

Thick

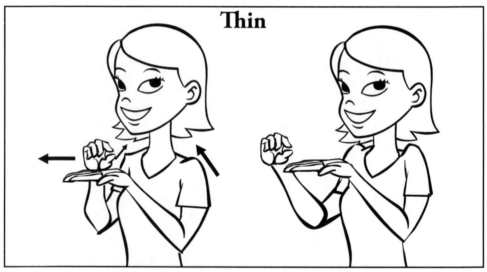

Thin

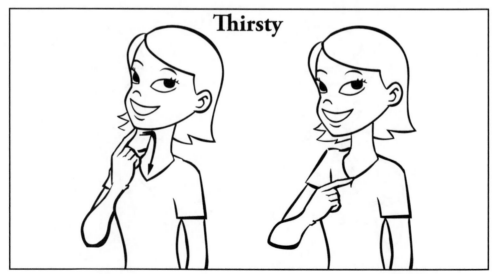

Thirsty

Throw Away

Thunder

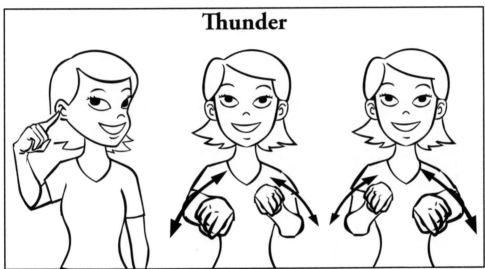

Ticket

Tie

Tiger

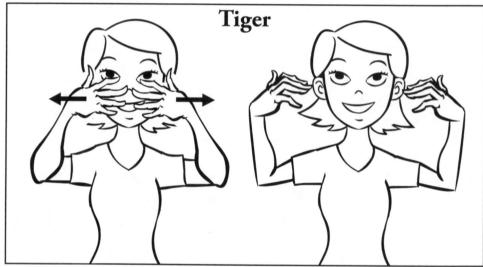

Time

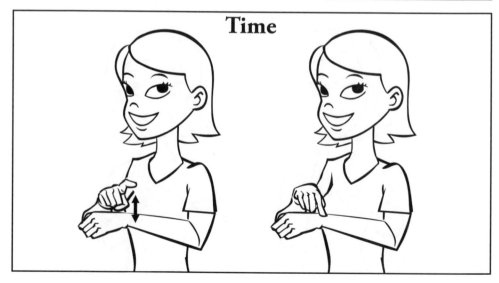

Tired

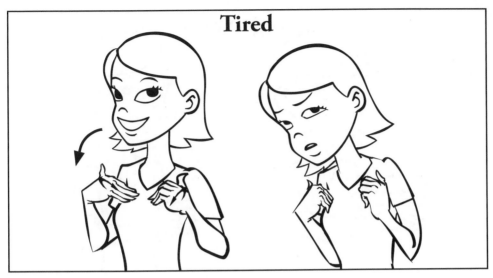

Tissue

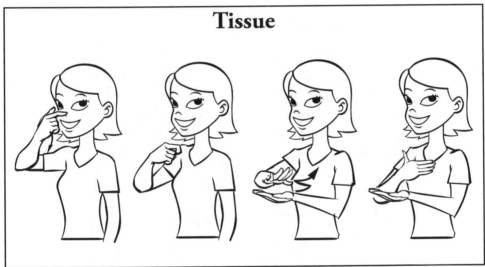

Toast

Together

Toilet (potty)

Tomato

Tools

Toothbrush (brush teeth)

Toothpaste

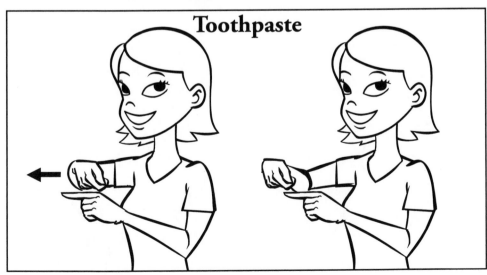

Touch

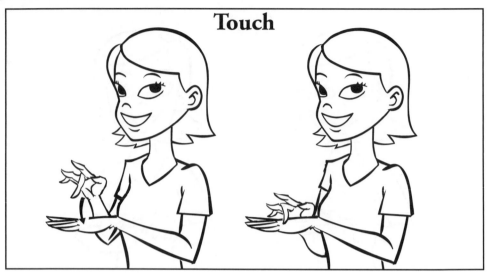

Towel

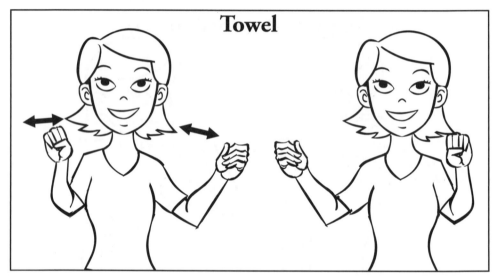

Toy

Train

Travel

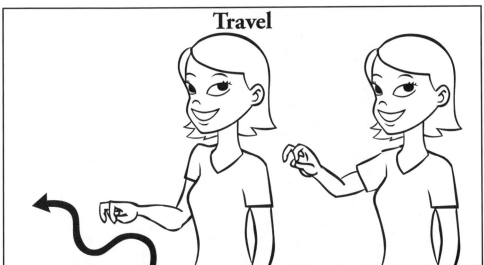

Tree

Triplet

Truck

Try

Turkey

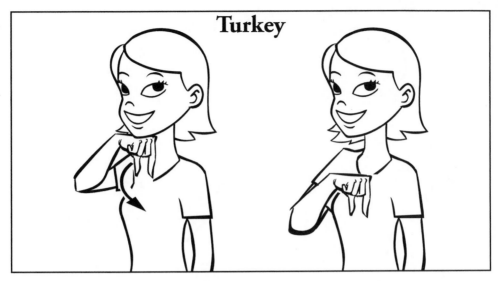

Turn (my)

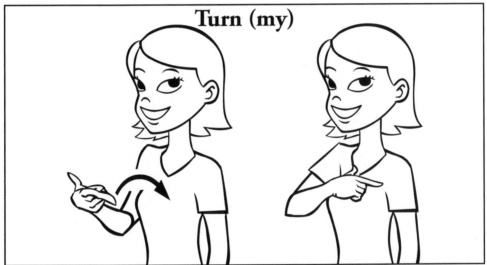

Turn (your)

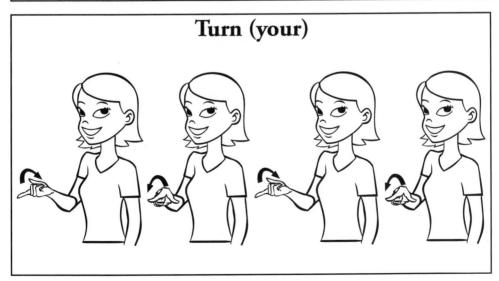

Turns (alternate)

Turtle

Twin

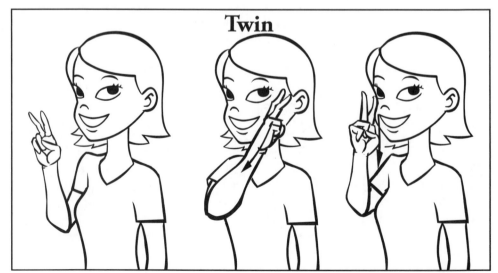

Uu

U

Ugly

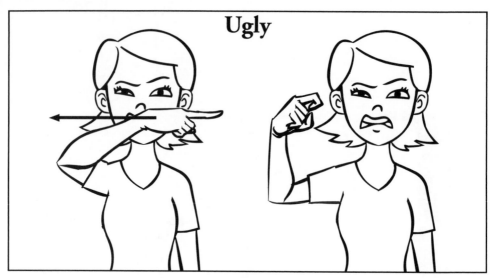

Umbrella

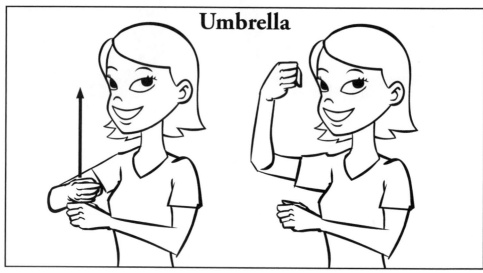

Uncle

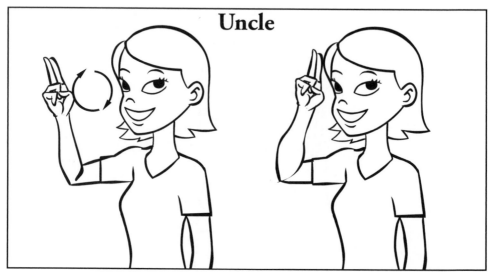

Under

Understand

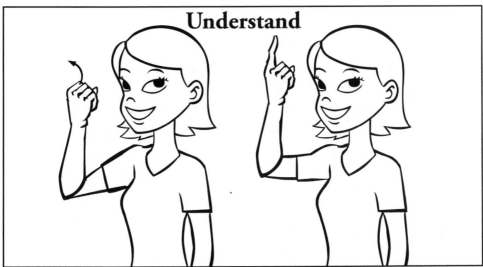

Undress

Unicorn

Up

Upstairs

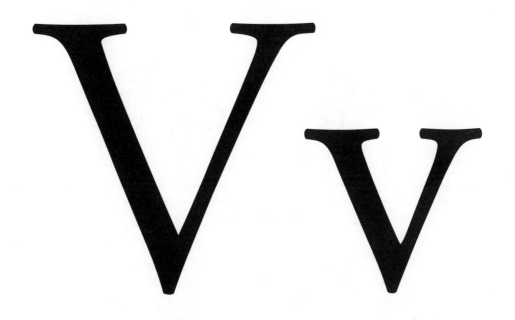

Vacuum

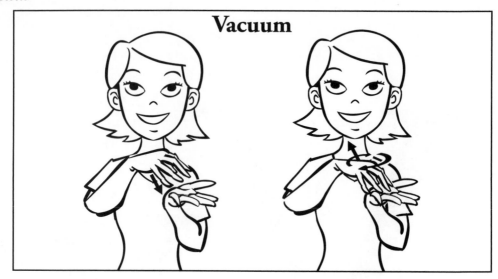

Vegetable

Vomit

W w

W

Wagon

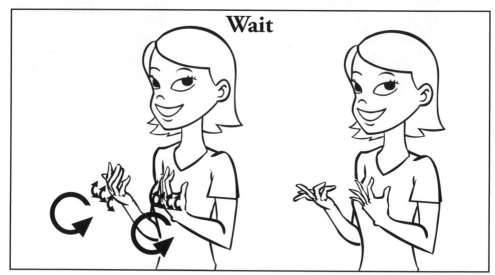

Wait

Wake Up

Walk

Wall

Want

Warm

Wash

Wash Hands

Watch

Water

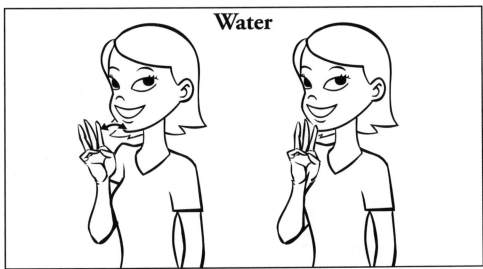

Watermelon

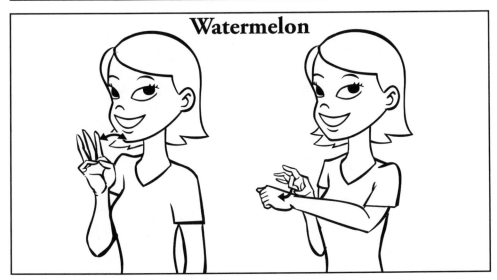

Wear

Wedding

Welcome

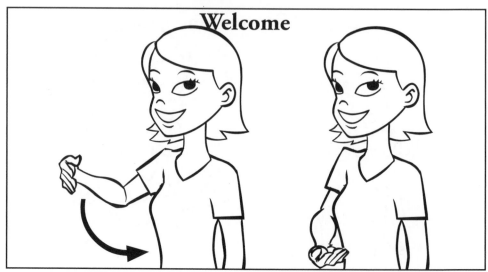

Wet

Whale

What

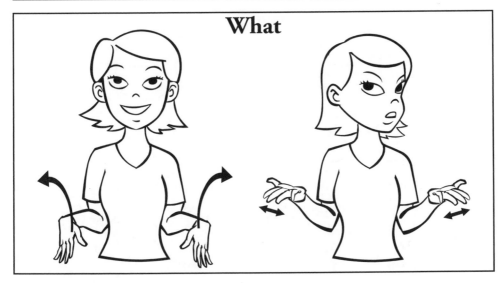

Wheel

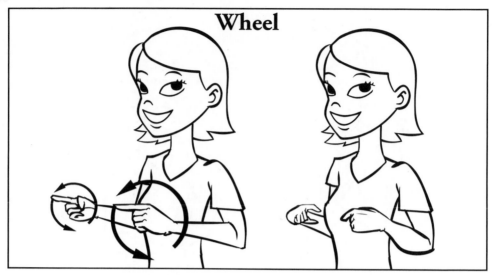

Wheelchair

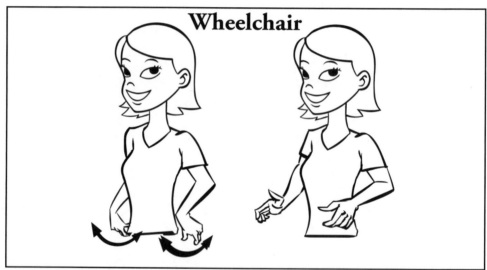

When

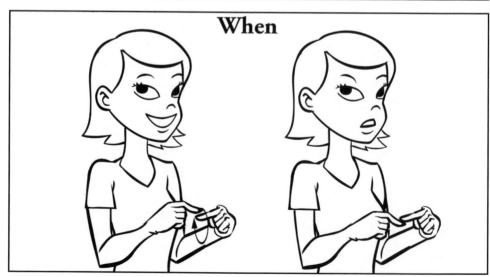

Where

Whisper

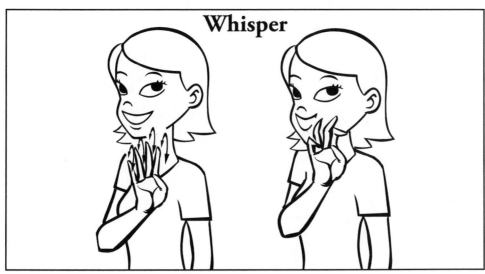

White

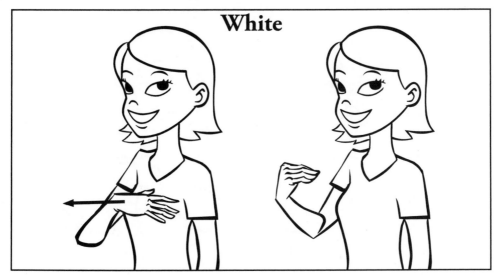

Who

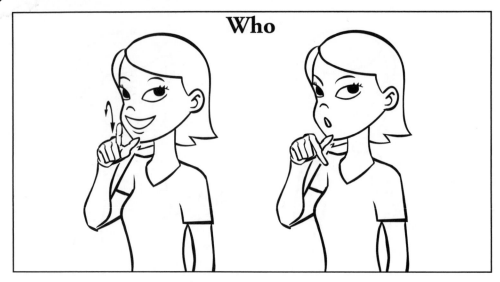

Why

Wind

Window

Wolf

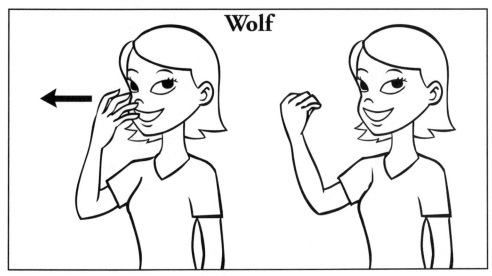

Woman

Wood

Word

Worm

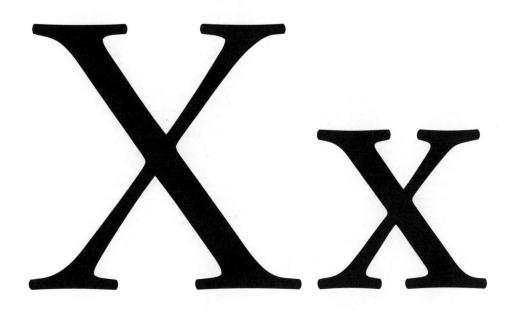

X

Xerox

X-ray

Xylophone

Y y

Y

Yard

Yarn

Yell

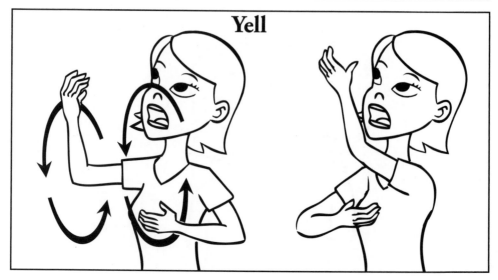

Yellow

Yes

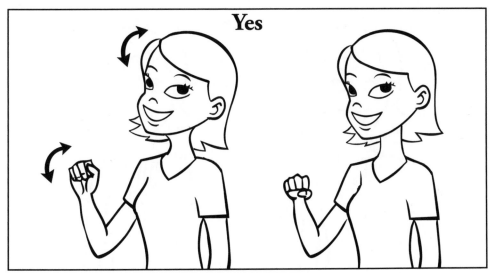

Yogurt

You're Welcome

Your

Yucky

Zz

z

Zebra

Zipper

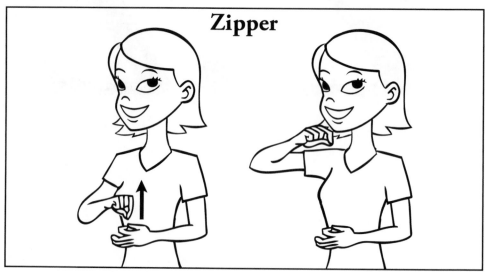

Zoo

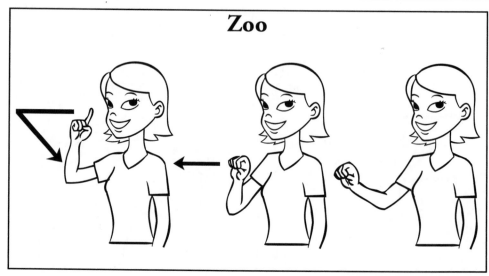

Numbers

Count

Number

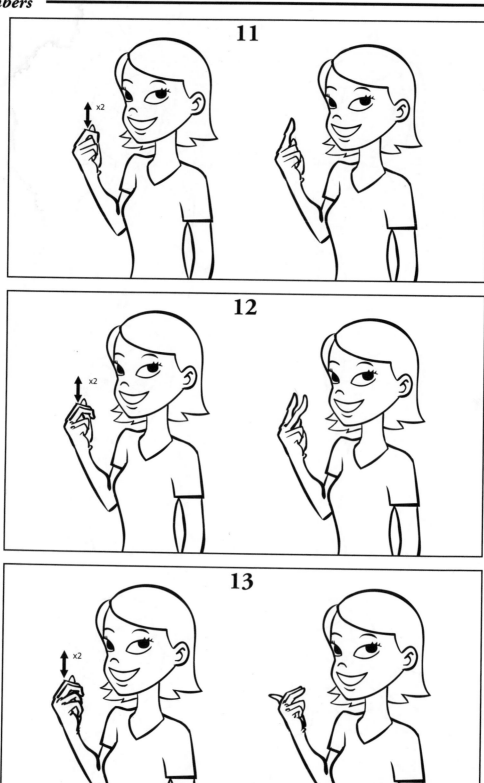

11

12

13